GRANTS
MADE EASY
YOUR FIRST STEPS

Quadira Dantro

Your Excellent Adventure
PO Box 75
Rockville, MD 94909
quadira@passionandprojects.com

Copyright © 2019 by Your Excellent Adventure, LLC

Ordering Information: Quantity sales. Special discounts are available on quantity purchases by corporations, associations, and others. For details, contact the publisher at the address above.

First Printing, 2019

ISBN Print   978-1-7338852-0-1
ISBN E-book   978-1-7338852-1-8

To my amazing husband, Dennis Dantro, who read and re-reread pieces of this book offering advice and content. When I waivered, he lit the spark to reinvigorate me. I am grateful for all of his love, support and friendship over the years. To my three beautiful children, thank you for reminding me of the true meaning of happiness. To my dear sisters, thank you for the love and inspiration.

TABLE OF CONTENTS

Over $600 billion in federal grants are awarded to small businesses, individuals, universities, states, and other organizations each year. Over the last several years, I've heard from more and more people about how hard it is to understand the grants process, and about how little information exists about what's involved in applying for and managing a grant. Lots of people have great ideas for a project, but do not know where to begin or what will be necessary. This book is here to help with details about the different steps involved in the application process, and to provide direct links to the information and resources that you'll need get started with applying for a federal grant.

This book won't tell you what to include in your application or how to make a compelling pitch for funds. That's your job—your pitch will be unique to your project.

That said, even though a grant for scientific research and a grant to help veterans get jobs don't seem to have much in common, information on competitive federal grants—no matter the subject—can be found in the same place. They share many of the same rules and forms, and they also require many of the same systems. This book will introduce you to the basic information that you'll need to find, apply for, and manage any competitive federal grant.

I think anyone should be able to apply for a grant, not just lawyers and lobbyists. With this book, anyone can learn answers to these common questions:

✔ HOW does the grant process work?

✔ WHAT do I need to do to apply for a federal grant?

✔ WHERE do I go to get started?

✔ WHAT resources exist to help with managing a grant?

This book answers those questions in a short and sweet format. It charts the path to applying for your grant, managing your grant, and closing your grant, all in plain English! It's time to simplify the grants management process.

What Is a Federal grant?

A grant is money provided by the government to a person or organization for ideas or projects that accomplish a public purpose. Grants are awarded for a variety of purposes such as scientific research, public health projects, childcare programs, and veterans reemployment programs. Applying for a federal grant is free.

A federal grant is not...

A gift from the government! Grants have rules, milestones, and government oversight.

Who makes grants?

Broadly, grants are made by states, local governments, non-profits, individuals, small business, and even major corporations. This book is focused on grants made by the federal government.

What's the difference between a federal contract and a federal grant?

A federal contract requires you to provide a service or product to the government; grants, on the other hand, require you to accomplish a goal that benefits the public.

What are the different types of grants?

This book is focused on competitive grants, but there are many different types of grants. Types of federal grants:

- ✔ Competitive grants
- ✔ Cooperative agreements
- ✔ Mandatory grants
  - ✔ Block grants
  - ✔ Formula grants

Competitive Grants

A competitive grant is awarded based on a competition. The government selects the winner of a discretionary grant based on merit and eligibility.

Applications for competitive grants go through a formal competitive review process at each government agency. Each agency decides on its own review process. The purpose of the review is to ensure that applications are reviewed fairly and consistently. Once the review process is complete, a decision is made on who will get an award.

While agencies often use a scoring process to rank applications, agencies may—and do—make decisions based on things other than a simple score. For example, an award may be made to a nonprofit childcare organization in a rural community because none of the higher-scoring applicants will serve that population.

When it comes to competitive grants, the government monitors the work performed by the grantee but does not participate in the performance of the project. Monitoring is usually done through periodic reports on the work being done, as well as methods like project site visits.

For example, if you receive a grant for $40,000 to set up an organic garden in your community, you will set up the garden on your own based on the plan that you submitted in your application, and then you will send in scheduled reports to the government on its progress and outcomes.

Environmental Quality Incentives Program

Environmental Quality
Incentives Program

From weather to pests, and from a lack of time to markets, each American farmer faces a unique set of challenges. The Environmental Quality Incentives Program (EQIP) helps agricultural producers confront those challenges – all while conserving natural resources like soil, water and air.

Cooperative Agreements

A cooperative agreement is the same as a grant except for one significant difference—cooperative agreements involve substantial involvement between the government and the grantee.

"Substantial involvement" means that government staff are involved in performing or implementing parts of the project. The amount of involvement depends on the program.

For example, if you receive a cooperative agreement for $40,000 to set up an organic garden in your community, you may need to work with the government official on specifics such as which vegetables to plant, the location of the garden, and the best time to harvest. Just like with competitive grants, you will also need to submit scheduled reports to the government on the project's progress and outcomes.

Mandatory Grants

Mandatory grants are grants that must be awarded based on law. Mandatory grants are generally awarded to U.S. state, local, or territory governments.

Types of Mandatory Grants:

Block grants

Block grants are usually based on a formula, and the money that is awarded has few strings attached as long as the purpose and parameters of the law are met. Block grant award recipients have lots of independence and flexibility to decide how to use the grant money.

The Community Development Block Grant is an example of a block grant. It is used to give money to communities for projects that help with affordable housing, sewer systems, and other initiatives such as redeveloping abandoned homes. The funds are distributed directly to states or cities, who then use their own process to distribute the money to their communities based on factors like community need, poverty level, and population.

Formula Grant

Formula grants are awarded for specific types of work based on statistical criteria and are made based on a formula that is set by laws and regulations.

Medicaid is a good example of a formula grants program. The government gives each state a mandatory grant for Medicaid based on a specific formula, as long as federal regulations are followed.

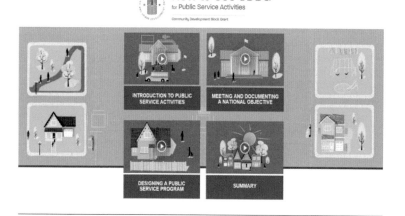

Grants Lifecycle

Now that we know about the types of grants, let's take a look at the grants lifecycle. It all begins with you!

You must first develop an idea for a project that can benefit the public. Once you have an idea in mind, you look for funding opportunity announcements and federal programs that align with what you have in mind. After you've found a Notice of Funding Opportunity (NOFO) that is accepting applications, you apply to enter the competition. (You can find NOFOs at www.Grants.gov; we'll talk about where and how to look for NOFOs in the upcoming sections.) If you're selected for an award, you will be given all of the details about the government requirements that you must follow to manage your grant responsibly. At the end of your project, you complete paperwork to explain what you've accomplished, and follow the official process to close out the award.

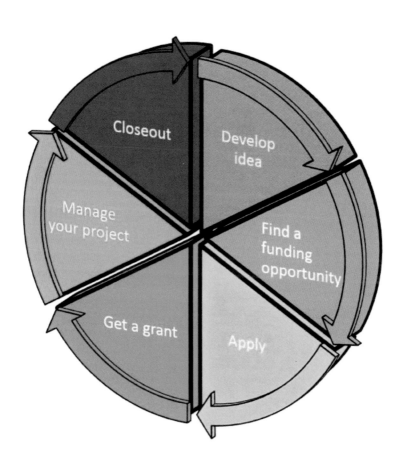

What Rules Do I Follow to Manage a Grant?

Many different rules apply to grants. They come in the form of laws, regulations, policies, terms, and conditions. A great place to start to learn the big picture is the Grants Uniform Guidance regulations, which can be found in the Code of Federal Regulation online here:

https://gov.ecfr.io/cgi-bin/
retrieveECFR?gp=1&SID=
85aeb03d66035b3befcf86202d705e00&ty=
HTML&h=l&mc=true&n=pt2.1.200&r=PART

The link takes you directly to the grants regulations at 2 CFR 200, which provides an in-depth set of rules that will help you to understand your responsibilities as a grantee and will apply to most grant programs.

PART 200—UNIFORM ADMINISTRATIVE REQUIREMENTS, COST PRINCIPLES, AND AUDIT REQUIREMENTS FOR FEDERAL AWARDS

Contents

Subpart A—Acronyms and Definitions

ACRONYMS

The regulations at 2 CFR 200 provide you with the basic grant requirements for federal grants in general. The NOFO will tell you exactly which laws, regulations, and policies apply to the program that you are interested in.

When you win a grant award, the NOA will also tell you what laws, regulations, and policies apply to your project, as well as any specific terms and conditions that apply to your award.

It is essential to review the rules that apply to the program, because failure to comply could result in your grant being terminated, financial penalty, and in some cases, jail time. The are no case officers assigned to your grant to assist you with compliance, so you'll have to work independently to ensure that you're following the rules.

Where Can I Learn About Specific Grant Programs?

General details about all federal grant programs can be found in the "Assistance Listings," a federal website that has searchable information about programs. You can access the site here: https://beta.sam.gov/search?index=cfda. Each grant program has a unique five-digit Catalog of Federal Domestic Assistance (CFDA) number that you can use to refer to the program. You can find details about every program's goals, objectives, past and estimated future funding, and, vitally, contact information for the government agency.

You can search the Assistance Listings for information about federal programs across the government using keywords and the five-digit CFDA number.

The Assistance Listings also include direct links to any of the NOFOs that are posted on Grants.gov!

Who Can Apply?

Each grant program's Notice of Funding Opportunity (NOFO) will let you know if you can apply. Always check the "Eligibility" section of NOFOs that interest you. Do not ever assume that you are not eligible, because you may be surprised! Here's an example list of eligible organizations from a NOFO published in 2018:

- ❑ County governments
- ❑ Nonprofits having a 501(c)(3) status with the IRS, other than institutions of higher education
- ❑ Independent school districts
- ❑ Public housing authorities/Indian housing authorities
- ❑ City or township governments
- ❑ Special district governments
- ❑ Native American tribal organizations (other than federally recognized tribal governments)
- ❑ Private institutions of higher education
- ❑ State governments
- ❑ Native American tribal governments (federally recognized)

To apply to the opportunities that interest you, you will need to register with a few different websites. Registering for all of the systems is free, so if you encounter any organizations or sites soliciting a fee or charge, do not use them—they are scams!

You'll need to keep track of a few screen names, passwords, email addresses, and phone numbers. You will likely be able to use the same accounts in the future, so it pays to keep good track of your account information.

I've created a checklist of the required steps and a chart showing how long each step takes.

I'm going to give you all of the information that you need to get this done with ease and confidence.

Stay organized, and it'll be a snap. Let's go!

Getting Started with the System for Award Management (SAM)

To apply for a Federal grant, you must register with the System for Award Management (SAM), which is generally just called SAM. SAM serves as the birthplace for all grant ambitions. In SAM, every organization is represented by a nine-digit unique-entity identifier.

To register in SAM, your organization must first have a Data Universal Numbering System (DUNS®) Number and an Employer Identification Number (EIN). If you're wondering, what are those????!!!! Don't worry.

They are numbers that you obtain by registering with other organizations.

In the case of the DUNS® Number, you'll be registering with the DUN and Bradstreet website, and in the case of the EIN, you will be registering with the Internal Revenue Service (IRS) website.

Let's learn more about both.

View assistance for SAM.gov

A NEW WAY TO SIGN IN - If you already have a SAM account, use your **SAM email** for login.gov.

Login.gov FAQs

HOME   SEARCH RECORDS   DATA ACCESS   CHECK STATUS   ABOUT   HELP

⚠ ALERT - June 11, 2018: Entities registering in SAM must submit a notarized letter appointing their authorized Entity Administrator. Read our updated FAQs to learn more about changes to the notarized letter review process and other system improvements.

⚠ ALERT - There may be a delay in data updates between the Small Business Administration (SBA) and SAM. If you notice any issues with your entity's SBA status or trouble on the SBA Supplemental page, please contact the Federal Service Desk.

⚠ ALERT - Direct hyperlinks to the Federal Acquisition Regulation (FAR) are not working due to Acquisition.gov maintenance. SAM.gov will restore all hyperlinks as soon as the FAR is restored on Acquisition.gov.

The System for Award Management (SAM) is an official website of the U.S. government. There is no cost to use SAM. You can use this site for FREE to:

- Register to do business with the U.S. government
- Update or renew your entity registration
- Check status of an entity registration
- Search for entity registration and exclusion records

Getting Started

Create A User Account

Start by creating a SAM user account.

Register Entity

After creating your SAM user account, log in to register to do business with the U.S. government.

Search Records

Do a public search for existing entity registration records or exclusion records.

Federal users can log in to see additional information.

GSA

Search Records	Disclaimers	FAPIIS.gov
Data Access	Accessibility	GSA.gov/IAE
Check Status	Privacy Policy	GSA.gov

Registering for a Data Universal Numbering System (DUNS®) Number

The Data Universal Numbering System (DUNS®) number is issued by a company called Dun & Bradstreet. It's a unique nine-digit character number used to identify your organization. The federal government uses the DUNS® number to track how federal money is spent.

If your organization does not have a DUNS® number, or if it might, but no one knows it, visit the Dun & Bradstreet (D&B) website here: http://fedgov.dnb.com/webform/displayHomePage.do or call 1-866-705-5711 to register or search for a DUNS® number. It can take up two business days to get a DUNS® number.

Have the following information handy to register for your DUNS® number:

- ☐ Name of organization

- ☐ Organization address

- ☐ Name of the Chief Executive Officer (CEO) or organization's owner

- ☐ Legal structure of the organization (e.g., corporation, partnership, proprietorship)

- ☐ Year the organization started

- ☐ Primary type of business

- ☐ Total number of employees (full- and part-time)

Registering for an Employer Identification Number (EIN)

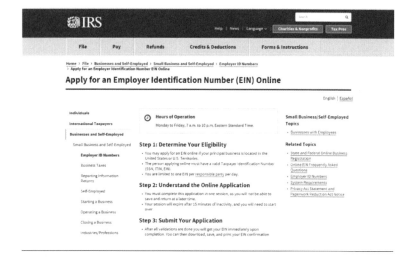

An Employer Identification Number (EIN) is an identification number used by the Internal Revenue Service (IRS) in the administration of tax laws. It is also known as a federal tax identification number. The EIN is used by the IRS to identify business entities.

You can apply for an EIN online here: https://www.irs.gov/businesses/small-businesses-self-employed/apply-for-an-employer-identification-number-ein-online.

You'll want to take a look at the website to check for any specific instructions that may apply to your situation; for example, employers located in Puerto Rico should use the following form to apply: Solicitud de Número de Identificación Patronal (EIN) SS-4PR (PDF).

Login.gov

Once you have those, the process for registering in SAM begins with creating a Login.Gov account.

Creating a Login.gov account is simple and begins here: https://secure.login.gov/sign_up/enter_email.

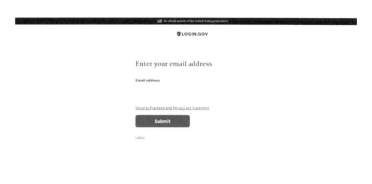

The website will walk you through a few simple steps to get registered and will send a code to your phone for verification. Login.gov requires all users to use two-factor authentication when creating an account and signing in, which requires a telephone number receiving a code. You can obtain the security code via a mobile phone or landline. Mobile phones can receive security codes by text message or phone call. Landlines can receive security codes only by a phone call. If you do not have a phone, you can also set up your account using the computer you are using to sign in.

Registering in SAM

Once your Login.gov account is set up, you can begin the next step to register in SAM. Make sure that you have your DUNS® and EIN handy and follow this link to SAM: https://www.sam.gov/SAM/. Once on the page, select the option to "Create a User Account" and then follow the system prompts to answer some questions about your organization.

EBIZ, MPIN & AOR, oh my!

During the SAM registration process, you will be required to designate someone as an EBiz Point of Contact (POC). That person will have the authority to make decisions for your organization.

The EBiz POC will be given a Marketing Personal Identification Number (MPIN) in SAM. This allows the EBiz POC to designate the Authorized Organization Representatives (AOR). The AORs are the people in your organization who can submit applications on Grants.gov.

We'll have more about Grants.gov later, but for now think of it as the home of NOFO postings.

The last part of the SAM registration process is the submission of a notarized letter appointing an "Authorized Entity Administrator." The Authorized Entity Administrator will serve as an authorized officer, agent, or representative of your entity. You should submit the letter after creating the individual account on the SAM website. This is important, because the Authorized Entity Administrator that you appoint must already have an individual user account in SAM, and the notarized letter will need to include the email address that you used to register.

A **template and a few tips** that you can follow are provided below.

Your registration in SAM can only be activated after the approved letter is on file.

Remember to:

✔ **Print the letter on your entity's letterhead.** If you don't have letterhead, enter your entity's legal business name and physical address at the top of the letter before printing.

✔ **Sign the completed letter in the presence of a notary.**

✔ Make sure that the person who signs the letter is someone who **can make commitments on behalf of your organization,** like an executive, officer, or partner.

TEMPLATE

[Insert Date]

FEDERAL SERVICE DESK
ATTN: SAM.GOV REGISTRATION PROCESSING
460 INDUSTRIAL BLVD
LONDON, KY 40741-7285
UNITED STATES OF AMERICA

SUBJECT: Information Required to Activate SAM Entity Registration

Purpose of Letter

The purpose of this letter is to formally appoint an Entity Administrator for the named entity and to attest to the accuracy of the information contained in the entity registration.

Designation of Entity Administrator

I, **[Insert Name and Title of Signatory]**, the below-signed individual, hereby confirm that the appointed Entity Administrator is an authorized officer, agent, or representative of the entity. This letter authorizes the appointed Entity Administrator to manage the entity's registration record, its associated users, and their roles to the entity, in the System for Award Management (SAM).

Entity Covered by This Letter

DUNS® Number: _____

Legal Business Name: _____

Physical Address: _____

Entity Administrator Contact Information

Full Name: _____

Phone Number: _____

Email Address: _____

Account Administration Preference (ONLY CHOOSE ONE)

** *Choose ONE of the two following statements by checking the applicable box.*

Remember, there is no cost to register in SAM— it is free. However, if you choose to have a third-party agent administer your SAM registration, with or without an associated fee, you must check the Third-Party Agent Designation box below.

❏ Self-Administration Confirmation

For the purpose of registering with the United States Government through the online System for Award Management (SAM), I do not authorize any third party to act on behalf of the entity listed above. I have checked the Self-Administration Confirmation box to indicate that the designated Entity Administrator is not a third-party agent.

❏ Third-Party Agent Designation

For the purpose of registering with the United States Government through the online System for Award Management (SAM), I do hereby authorize **[insert full name, phone number, address, and email address of the Third-Party Agent]** (Designated Third-Party Agent) to act on behalf of the entity listed above. This authorization permits the Designated Third-Party Agent to conduct all normal, common business functions within SAM while binding the signatory to all actions conducted and representations made as a result of authorization granted herein. I have checked the Third-Party Agent Designation box and completed the above information to indicate that the designated Entity Administrator is a third-party agent.

Attestation

I, the below-signed, attest to the following:

- ✔ All information contained in this letter is complete and accurate.

- ✔ The designated Entity Administrator listed above has an individual SAM User Account created with the email address provided in this letter.

- ✔ The banking information provided for Electronic Funds Transfer on the Financial Information Page in the SAM.gov registration for the entity above is correct and accurate.

Respectfully,

[Insert Full Name of Signatory]

[Insert Title of Signatory, e.g. Director of Contracting, Managing Partner, Vice President for Research, etc.]

[Insert Email of Signatory]

[Insert Entity Legal Business Name]

[Insert Entity Physical Address]

Once you've completed your application in the system and submitted your notarized letter, your submission will be reviewed, and you will either receive follow-up questions or confirmation of registration.

Generally, after completing the online registration and sending your notarized letter confirming the Entity Administrator, **it takes up to two weeks for a registration to be completed,** and then **one additional business day for updates made in SAM** to be reflected in the system that is used to apply for grants, Grants.gov.

Once your SAM registration is complete, you will be able to proceed with applying for a grant!

To keep your SAM account active, you will need to renew each year.

Grants.gov

Grants.gov is where you go to find NOFOs for active and forecasted grants opportunities.

Opportunities are posted there for more than 1,000 different grant programs that will award more than $500 billion annually.

The site is a one-stop shop to find open grant opportunities, learn application requirements, see who's eligible for a NOFO, and learn details about the application process.

Register with Grants.gov

Anyone can browse around on Grants.gov to see open funding opportunities, but to apply to a NOFO, you will need to register. You must have your DUNS® number and EIN ready, and your SAM registration completed.

You'll only have to register once to apply to as many federal agencies and grant programs as you want.

To get started, visit https://www.grants.gov/web/ grants/register.html and complete the on-screen instructions to set up your account.

The Grants.gov registration process is simple, and the account is usually approved by the website within one day.

Search for Notices of Funding Opportunities (NOFO)

Once you're on the Grants.gov website, you can search for Notices of Funding Opportunities (NOFO) using a simple keyword or do more advanced searches using the functions on the site, which include exploring by government agency and grant category.

Use the search box in the top right-hand corner of the page to see opportunities that are posted and forecasted.

Click on a link to a NOFO to access details about the opportunity.

When you click on an individual NOFO, details about the opportunity will be displayed. When you're reviewing an open opportunity, the "Current Closing Date for Applications," on the upper right-hand side of the page, tells you the last date on which applications will be accepted.

Review the NOFO very carefully to learn whether a specific opportunity is right for you. Check the dates, eligibility, and description first and foremost to find out if you should proceed with a deeper dive into the details. If your quick look lets you know that this is an opportunity that you'd like to pursue, you can access more detailed information in the "Related Documents" tab.

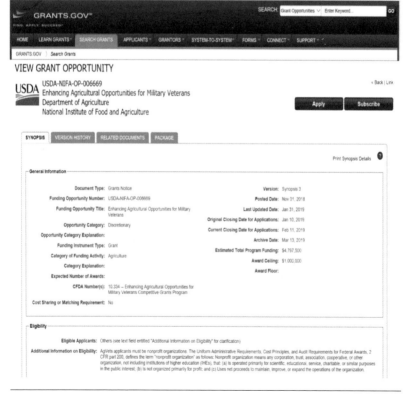

Once you're registered with Grants.gov, you can subscribe to have all sorts of grants information sent to you directly.

Use this link to sign up based on your preferences: https://www.grants.gov/manage-subscriptions.html

Options to Obtain Grants Information Include:

✔ **Subscribe to Grants.gov News:**

Receive Alerts and Newsletters containing updates about system enhancements and training resources.

✔ **Subscribe to all new grant opportunities:**

Receive a daily email listing all new grant opportunities.

✔ **Subscribe to opportunities:**

Receive notifications when changes are made to a specific opportunity's forecast, synopsis, and/or packages.

✔ **Subscribe to saved searches for grant opportunities:**

Receive notifications for new opportunities matching saved search criteria.

Beginner's Guide to Grants Checklist

- ❏ Familiarize yourself with the Federal Grants Lifecycle

- ❏ Get a DUNS® number

- ❏ Get an EIN

- ❏ Register with LOGIN.GOV

- ❏ Register with SAM.Gov
    - ❏ Send notarized letter

- ❏ Register with Grants.gov

- ❏ Search Grants.gov to see what opportunities are available and then:

    - ❏ Determine your eligibility for a program
    - ❏ Review the rules and laws that apply to the program
    - ❏ Review the milestone requirements for the program

- ❏ Review the reporting requirements for the award

- ❏ Apply for a grant!

How long does each step take?

Required Step	Typical Time Required
EIN	2 weeks
DUNS® number	2 days
Login.gov	1 day
SAM.gov	2 weeks
Grants.gov	1 day
Search NOFOs	Daily
Apply	1 month

Applying for a Grant

Completing the grant application takes time, but the format that you will need to follow is simple. Details on how to apply will be included in the NOFO that is posted on Grants.gov.

Every NOFO will require the submission of an application, which will include a standard form that must be used. If you'd like to look at some of the standard forms that may be required, go to this website: https://www.grants.gov/web/grants/forms/forms-repository.html.

The purpose of the application form is to gather critical information about the organization that is applying and what they intend to do if selected for funding. For example, applicants will be asked to provide details about the organization, a description of the proposed project, milestones, and a proposed project budget. Here's an example:

APPLICATION FOR FEDERAL DOMESTIC ASSISTANCE - Short Organizational

7. PROJECT DIRECTOR

Prefix:	* First Name:	Middle Name:

* Last Name:	Suffix:

* Title:	* Email:

* Telephone Number:	Fax Number:

* Street1:	Street2:

* City:	County/Parish:

* State:	Province:

* Country:	* Zip/Postal Code:

8. PRIMARY CONTACT/GRANTS ADMINISTRATOR

☐ Same as Project Director (skip to item 9):

Prefix:	* First Name:	Middle Name:

* Last Name:	Suffix:

* Title:	* Email:

* Telephone Number:	Fax Number:

* Street1:	Street2:

* City:	County/Parish:

* State:	Province:

* Country:	* Zip/Postal Code:

In many cases, you will be able to save your work as you complete the forms. You will need to provide necessary information, like organization title, address, details about the proposed project, and financial data.

Drafting the narrative part of a grant application, in which you describe your plan's details, can take two weeks or more depending on the application's requirements and the complexity of your proposal.

Once you've completed the application package, you can usually submit it through the Grants.gov website. Application instructions will be included in the NOFO.

The tracking process for applications is unique to each agency. To keep track of your application, you will need to reach out to the government agency that will be awarding the grants. The contact information is included in each NOFO.

The Notice of Award (NOA)

The Notice of Award (NOA) is the official, legally binding document, signed by a Grants Management Official that:

1. Lets you know that you are being awarded a grant;

2. Contains or references all the terms and conditions of the grant, as well as federal funding limits and obligations; and,

3. Notifies the recipient that funds may be requested from the designated payment system or office.

It includes the following information:

✔ Grant number

✔ Federal award date

✔ Approved start and end dates

✔ Total amount of the federal award

✔ Applicable terms and conditions of the award, either by reference or inclusion

- ✔ Award performance goals

- ✔ Any restriction on the use of funds

- ✔ Name(s) of senior personnel

- ✔ Your Grants Management Official and Program Points of Contact.

PMS DOCUMENT NUMBER:

1. AWARDING OFFICE:		2. ASSISTANCE TYPE: Discretionary Grant	3. AWARD NO.:	4. AMEND. NO. 0
5. TYPE OF AWARD: Other		6. TYPE OF ACTION: New	7. AWARD AUTHORITY:	
8. BUDGET PERIOD: THRU		9. PROJECT PERIOD: THRU		
11. RECIPIENT ORGANIZATION:			12. PROJECT / PROGRAM TITLE:	
13. COUNTY:	14. CONGR. DIST:		15. PRINCIPAL INVESTIGATOR OR PROGRAM DIRECTOR:	

16. APPROVED BUDGET:		17. AWARD COMPUTATION:		
Personnel	$ 50,000.00	A. NON-FEDERAL SHARE .... $	20,000.00	20%
Fringe Benefits	$ 30,000.00	B. FEDERAL SHARE .... $	80,000.00	80%
Travel	$ 0.00	18. FEDERAL SHARE COMPUTATION:		
		A. TOTAL FEDERAL SHARE .... $		80,000.00
Equipment	$ 0.00	B. UNOBLIGATED BALANCE FEDERAL SHARE ...... $		0.00
Supplies	$ 0.00	C. FED. SHARE AWARDED THIS BUDGET PERIOD ..$		0.00
Contractual	$ 0.00	19. AMOUNT AWARDED THIS ACTION:	$	80,000.00
Facilities/Construction	$ 0.00	20. FEDERAL $ AWARDED THIS PROJECT PERIOD:	$	80,000.00
Other	$ 20,000.00			
Direct Costs	$ 100,000.00	21. AUTHORIZED TREATMENT OF PROGRAM INCOME: Additional Costs		
Indirect Costs At % of $	$ 0.00			
In Kind Contributions	$ 0.00	22. APPLICANT EIN:	23. PAYEE EIN:	24. OBJECT CLASS:
Total Approved Budget	$ 100,000.00			

25. FINANCIAL INFORMATION:					DUNS	
ORGN	DOCUMENT NO.	APPROPRIATION	CAN NO.	NEW AMT. $80,000.00	UNOBLIG.	NONFED %

26. REMARKS: (Continued on separate sheets)

New award for $80,000.00

27. SIGNATURE - GRANTS OFFICER	DATE:	28. SIGNATURE(S) CERTIFYING FUND AVAILABILITY
29. SIGNATURE AND TITLE - PROGRAM OFFICIAL(S)		DATE:

Grant Management Official and Program Official

You NOA will include contact information that you can use to stay in touch with the government agency that gave you the grant award.

It's good to communicate with your POCs routinely, especially if questions arise and you need advice on the proper way to manage an issue related to your grant award.

They will be the source of information about the terms and conditions of your grant award.

Also, you should notify them immediately of significant changes to the project, such as those impacting the use of funds, the loss of primary staff, or any issue that will affect your ability to complete the project.

There are two primary POCs, your Grants Management Official and your Program Official.

Grants Management Official

Your Grants Management Official handles the business and administrative aspects of the award. This includes your grant award negotiation, reporting, budgeting, and management.

Work with your Grants Management Official on:

✔ Questions about your budget

✔ Questions about any terms and conditions on your NOA

✔ Clarification of grant policies

✔ Delay in completing paperwork required to issue your award

✔ Any change to the project that will require prior approval

Program Official

Your Program Official will be your point of contact for the programmatic and technical aspects of your grant.

The PO's responsibilities include:

- ✔ Development of grants programs

- ✔ Assisting with questions about program goals

- ✔ Setting and reviewing milestones

- ✔ Review of progress reports

- ✔ Participation in site visits

The PO and the GMO work as a team on many of these activities.

Accepting a Grant Award

Y ou indicate acceptance of an award and its associated terms and conditions by requesting funds from the payment system or office, but in some cases, you are required to respond to your NOA in writing to indicate acceptance. Acceptance of a federal grant creates **a legal obligation to use the funds** per the terms and conditions of the grant. If for some reason you cannot accept the award, notify the GMO immediately.

Once you accept the award, you assume full responsibility for the conduct of project activities and become accountable for meeting federal standards regarding:

- ✔ financial management
- ✔ internal controls
- ✔ audits
- ✔ reporting

You must have a solid accounting structure in place to provide accurate and complete information about all grant-related financial transactions.

Internal Controls

When you accept a federal grant, it is important to have processes within your organization to help ensure that your objectives will be achieved. These are commonly referred to as "Internal Controls." Internal Controls are the plans, methods, policies, and procedures used to guide the fulfillment of your mission, strategic plan, goals, and objectives.

They are essential because they are your primary defense against waste and misuse. They are crucial for good stewardship of your federal grant funds — and your organization's resources.

The government has an excellent resource to help with the design, implementation, and use of internal controls. It's called the "Green Book," and it can be accessed here: https://www.gao.gov/assets/670/665712.pdf, or here: www.gao.gov/green-book

What is the Green Book and how is it used?

Important facts and concepts related to the Green Book and internal control

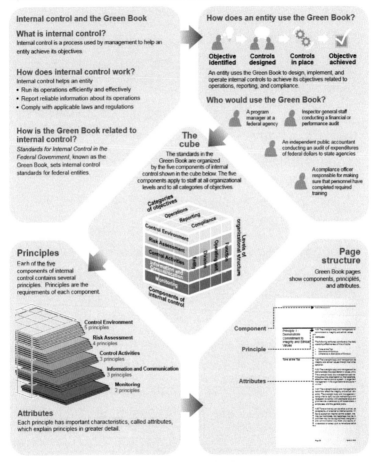

Internal control and the Green Book

What is internal control?
Internal control is a process used by management to help an entity achieve its objectives.

How does internal control work?
Internal control helps an entity
- Run its operations efficiently and effectively
- Report reliable information about its operations
- Comply with applicable laws and regulations

How is the Green Book related to internal control?
Standards for Internal Control in the Federal Government, known as the Green Book, sets internal control standards for federal entities.

How does an entity use the Green Book?

| Objective identified | Controls designed | Controls in place | Objective achieved |

An entity uses the Green Book to design, implement, and operate internal controls to achieve its objectives related to operations, reporting, and compliance.

Who would use the Green Book?

A program manager at a federal agency

Inspector general staff conducting a financial or performance audit

An independent public accountant conducting an audit of expenditures of federal dollars to state agencies

A compliance officer responsible for making sure that personnel have completed required training

The cube
The standards in the Green Book are organized by the five components of internal control shown in the cube below. The five components apply to staff at all organizational levels and to all categories of objectives.

Categories of objectives
Operations
Reporting
Compliance

Control Environment
Risk Assessment
Control Activities
Information and Communication
Monitoring
Components of internal control

Levels of organizational structure

Principles
Each of the five components of internal control contains several principles. Principles are the requirements of each component.

Control Environment
5 principles

Risk Assessment
4 principles

Control Activities
3 principles

Information and Communication
3 principles

Monitoring
2 principles

Attributes
Each principle has important characteristics, called attributes, which explain principles in greater detail.

Page structure
Green Book pages show components, principles, and attributes.

Component

Principle

Attributes

GAO.GOV/GREENBOOK

GAO-14-704G

Managing Accounting Records

Your grants accounting records must be maintained on a current basis and balanced monthly.

The records must be supported by source documentation such as canceled checks, invoices, contracts, travel reports, donor letters, in-kind contribution reports, and personnel activity reports.

The same costs cannot be claimed and reported on more than one federal grant.

Your records must be preserved for three years following submission of the final Federal Financial Report (FFR) or payment request (whichever is later).

Actively review the grant regulations at 2 CFR Part 200, and the terms and conditions of the grant award, to check whether costs are reasonable, allowable, and properly allocated. If you're not sure, reach out to your Grants Management Official.

General Award Management Tips

✔ Make sure that your staffing costs are supported by proper documentation. For example, your staffing activity reports should show the actual activity of each employee who was paid with grant funds.

✔ Your financial management system should have adequate internal controls in place. For example, make sure that you have proper procedures in place to compare the actual expenditures with the budget.

✔ Spend advances of federal funds promptly. Once you draw down federal funds for your grant project, you should spend those funds within three days.

✔ Ensure that your reported grant project costs agree with your accounting records. For example, the Federal Financial Report should be prepared directly from worksheets reconciled to the accounts.

✔ Sustain documentation to support the amount charged to your grant for overhead (indirect) costs that benefitted all projects and activities of the organization.

✔ Check to see if you have any liability with the Internal Revenue Service. Until the debt has been paid or an agreement has been reached with the IRS, the government cannot make any payments to you or award you any new grants.

Accessing Your Funds

You will need to register with a federal payment system to get access to your grants funds and file financial reports. There are multiple payment systems. Details about two of them are included below.

One is the Payment Management System (PMS), a tool to help grantees draw down funds and file the required Federal Financial Report (FFR). You can view the PMS website here: https://pms.psc.gov/.

Other systems include the National Science Foundation's Award Cash Management $ervice (ACM$). NSF disburses funds to your organization's bank account based on the banking information submitted to SAM. Before requesting a payment transaction, make sure that your SAM registration is active and up to date, including the banking data. The system cannot make payments to grantees without an active SAM registration. You can view the website here: https://www.research.gov/research-portal/appmanager/base/desktop?_nfpb=true&_pageLabel=research_node_display&_nodePath=/researchGov/Service/Desktop/AwardCashManagementService.html

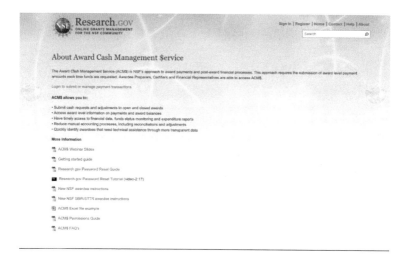

Federal Financial Report (FFR)

Once you are awarded a grant, you will need to report and account for your financial expenditures. Specifically, you will need to submit the mandatory Federal Financial Report (FFR), the SF-425.

The SF-425 is a standard form that is used to report cumulative expenses (calculated by adding all expenses, from the beginning of the grant to date; this includes overhead costs) incurred under the grant.

While the FFR is required on an annual basis (unless your NOA requires more frequent or less frequent reporting), you will be required to report the cash transaction data (items 10a-c) every quarter.

Federal Cash Transaction Report (FCTR)

The Federal Cash Transaction Report (FCTR) portion of the FFR must be filed within 30 days of the end of each of the following quarter-end dates:

- ✔ December 31 (1st Quarter of fiscal year)
- ✔ March 31 (2nd Quarter of fiscal year)
- ✔ June 30 (3rd Quarter of fiscal year)
- ✔ September 30 (4th Quarter of fiscal year)

If the FCTR is not filed before or on the due date, you will not be able to access funds.

You will be using the report to provide information about expenditures, outlays, and unobligated balances. You will also give information on any authorized extensions during the reported budget period.

The SF-425 form is provided below and can be found here: https://obamawhitehouse.archives.gov/sites/default/files/omb/grants/approved_forms/SF-425.pdf

You can also access detailed instructions for completing the form here: https://obamawhitehouse. archives.gov/sites/default/files/omb/grants/ standard_forms/SF-425_instructions.pdf

OMB Number: 4040-0014
Expiration Date 01/31/2019

Federal Financial Report
(Follow form instructions)

1. Federal Agency and Organizational Element to Which Report is Submitted	2. Federal Grant or Other Identifying Number Assigned by Federal Agency (To report multiple grants, use FFR Attachment)

3. Recipient Organization (Name and complete address including Zip code)

Recipient Organization Name:	
Street1:	
Street2:	
City:	County:
State:	Province:
Country:	ZIP / Postal Code:

4a. DUNS Number	4b. EIN	5. Recipient Account Number or Identifying Number (To report multiple grants, use FFR Attachment)

6. Report Type	7. Basis of Accounting	8. Project/Grant Period	9. Reporting Period End Date
☐ Quarterly	☐ Cash	From: To:	
☐ Semi-Annual	☐ Accrual		
☐ Annual			
☐ Final			

10. Transactions	Cumulative
(Use lines a-c for single or multiple grant reporting)	
Federal Cash (To report multiple grants, also use FFR attachment):	
a. Cash Receipts	
b. Cash Disbursements	
c. Cash on Hand (line a minus b)	
(Use lines d-o for single grant reporting)	
Federal Expenditures and Unobligated Balance:	
d. Total Federal funds authorized	
e. Federal share of expenditures	
f. Federal share of unliquidated obligations	
g. Total Federal share (sum of lines e and f)	
h. Unobligated balance of Federal Funds (line d minus g)	
Recipient Share:	
i. Total recipient share required	
j. Recipient share of expenditures	
k. Remaining recipient share to be provided (line i minus j)	
Program Income:	
l. Total Federal program income earned	
m. Program Income expended in accordance with the deduction alternative	
n. Program Income expended in accordance with the addition alternative	
o. Unexpended program income (line l minus line m or line n)	

11. Indirect Expense

a. Type	b. Rate	c. Period From	Period To	d. Base	e. Amount Charged	f. Federal Share
			g. Totals			

12. Remarks: Attach any explanations deemed necessary or information required by Federal sponsoring agency in compliance with governing legislation:

[Add Attachment] [Delete Attachment] [View Attachment]

13. Certification: By signing this report, I certify that it is true, complete, and accurate to the best of my knowledge. I am aware that any false, fictitious, or fraudulent information may subject me to criminal, civil or administrative penalties. (U.S. Code, Title 18, section 1001)

a. Name and Title of Authorized Certifying Official

Prefix: [___▾] First Name: [_____]   Middle Name: [_____]

Last Name: [_____]   Suffix: [___▾]

Title: [_____]

b. Signature of Authorized Certifying Official	c. Telephone (Area code, number and extension)

d. Email Address	e. Date Report Submitted	14. Agency use only:

Standard Form 425

Suspension and Debarment

Grants management rules include tools to address waste, fraud, abuse, poor performance, noncompliance, and other misconduct. These tools include the ability to suspend and/or debar individuals and entities. You can learn a great deal about this from the grants regulations at 2 CFR Part 180 by following this link: https://www.ecfr.gov/cgi-bin/text-idx?SID=0b1c0e993cf9c9bcd9d2c3a892e-97be2&node=pt2.1.180&rgn=div5

In essence, these protections protect the government (and taxpayer dollars) from recipients who pose a business risk to the government.

Once a person or organization is suspended or debarred, they are prevented from getting government contracts, subcontracts, loans, grants, and other assistance programs for the duration of the suspension or debarment period. The length of the period is determined on a case-by-case basis. The effect of suspension and debarment by a federal agency applies government-wide and cannot be appealed.

Audits

If your organization spends $750,000 or more in grants a year, you must have a single or program-specific audit conducted. So, what exactly is a single audit?

It's a review of the way your organization has managed your federal grant. The goal is to ensure that you are complying with the rules that apply to your award. The required components of an audit include such things as financial statements and records, expenditures, and internal controls.

You can review the rules and components of an audit in 2 CFR 200 by following this link:

https://gov.ecfr.io/cgi-bin/retrieveECFR?gp=1&SID =85aeb03d66035b3befcf86202d705e00&ty= HTML&h=L&mc=true&n=pt2.1.200&r= PART#sp2.1.200.f.

Progress Reports

Progress reports are required annually for active grants. In some cases, you will be required to report more frequently. You will use the progress report to provide updates on the status of the project, updates on the money that has been spent, and when applicable, details about plans for the next year of the award.

The progress report will also be the place to provide updates on the specific milestones required for the project. The details that you provide will explain which of them have been met, which are pending, and whether there are any anticipated issues with meeting any milestones.

The Grants Management Official assigned to your award will provide information on how, when, and where to submit progress reports.

PERFORMANCE PROGRESS REPORT
SF-PPR

		Page	of Pages
1. Federal Agency and Organization Element to Which Report is Submitted	2. Federal Grant or Other Identifying Number Assigned by Federal Agency	3a. DUNS Number	
		3b. EIN	
4. Recipient Organization (Name and complete address including zip code)		5. Recipient Identifying Number or Account Number	

6. Project/Grant Period		7. Reporting Period End Date	8. Final Report? ☐ Yes ☐ No
Start Date: *(Month, Day, Year)*	End Date: *(Month, Day, Year)*	*(Month, Day, Year)*	9. Report Frequency ☐ annual ☐ semi-annual ☐ quarterly ☐ other *(If other, describe: _____)*

10. Performance Narrative   *(attach performance narrative as instructed by the awarding Federal Agency)*

11. Other Attachments   *(attach other documents as needed or as instructed by the awarding Federal Agency)*

12. Certification: I certify to the best of my knowledge and belief that this report is correct and complete for performance of activities for the purposes set forth in the award documents.

12a. Typed or Printed Name and Title of Authorized Certifying Official	12c. Telephone *(area code, number and extension)*
	12d. Email Address
12b. Signature of Authorized Certifying Official	12e. Date Report Submitted *(Month, Day, Year)*
	13. Agency use only

Making Changes to Your Project

You may want or need to make changes to your project after you receive the award. You may, for example, need to make a change to the budget or milestone dates to be successful in the long run. The terms and conditions included in your NOA will let you know which types of changes will require you to submit a request beforehand and which changes you can make independently.

Failure to obtain prior approval when it is required might result in disallowance of costs, termination of the award, or other enforcement action.

The Grants Management Official assigned to your award will provide information on how to submit a request for approval. The following page provides examples of changes that require prior approval and some examples of the information that you should include with your request.

Examples of Changes That May Require Prior Approval	
Change to Project	**Information to Include with Request**
Change to the Project's Budget	✔ Reason for requested change ✔ Impact on other aspects of the budget and project
Change in Key Personnel	✔ Why the change(s) are needed ✔ How project duties will be managed ✔ Effective date ✔ Replacement's resume
Project Extension	✔ Revised timeline ✔ Requested new end date

Closeout

Once your award is over, you will need to complete the official closeout process. To close out a grant, you need to submit programmatic and financial reports, which include:

- ✔ Final FFR
- ✔ Final Progress Report
- ✔ Final Invention Statement
- ✔ Equipment Inventory Report

If additional reports are required, they will be identified in the terms and conditions of the NOA.

All closeout reports are due 90 days after the period of performance end date. Failure to submit timely and accurate reports may affect future funding.

Also, even after an award is closed out, you must return money that is due to the government as a result of later refunds, corrections, or other transactions.

Congress has begun paying close attention to how federal agencies manage the grants closeout process over the last several years. As a result, agencies have been required to send a report to Congress providing details about any grants that haven't been closed out on time. The reporting requirements are outlined in the Grants Oversight and New Efficiency (GONE) Act. You can access the GONE Act to learn more about the requirements here:

https://www.congress.gov/114/plaws/publ117/PLAW-114publ117.pdf.

By: Dennis Dantro

An examination of the historical timeline of grants reveals that they are almost as old as the U.S. government itself. On July 16, 1778, President John Adams signed the "Relief of Sick and Disabled Seamen," which authorized the deduction of twenty cents per month from a seaman's wages for the sole purpose of funding medical care for sick and disabled seamen, as well as building additional hospitals for the seamen's treatment. The Act included merchant seaman, not just U.S. Navy seaman, and was the forerunner to today's U.S. Public Health Service. In 1871, President Ulysses S. Grant appointed the first Supervising Surgeon, now called the Surgeon General, and in 1887 a one-room laboratory on Staten Island dedicated to disease research became a very early precursor to the National Institutes of Health (NIH).

In 1979, the Department of Education Organization Act drafted by the 96th Congress, and signed into law by President Jimmy Carter, provided for the Department of Education and renamed the Department of Health, Education, and Welfare (HEW) the Department of Health and Human Services (HHS).

While today's modern grant system is mostly known for its cash outlays and financial assistance programs, grant programs were most known as donations of land to the states, known as land grants. Begun under the Articles of Confederation, which were in force from March 1, 1781, and continuing after the ratification of the United States Constitution, on June 21, 1788, Congress authorized federal land to states. By 1827, Ohio had received more than 90,000 acres to auction off to raise revenue for road improvements. In 1841, Ohio, Indiana, Illinois, Alabama, Missouri, Mississippi, Louisiana, Arkansas, and Michigan all received at least 500,000 acres of federal land to be auctioned to support various transportation projects. By 1900, Congress had donated 3.2 million acres of federal land to support road construction, 37.8 million acres for railroad improvements, and 64 million acres for flood control. In 1902 there were five federal grants to states and local governments: teaching materials for the blind, agricultural experiment stations, the care of disabled veterans, resident instruction in the land grant colleges, and funding to the District of Columbia with a total outlay of about $7 million.

Congress began to increase the number of grants again in response to the Great Depression when social concerns and the Vietnam War took precedence.

Under President Franklin Roosevelt's emergency relief programs characterized as the New Deal to combat the Great Depression, Congress enacted 16 new grants between 1933 and 1938. The cost of government grants increased from $214 million in 1932 to $790 million in 1938. The most well-known of the new grant programs was the Social

Security Act of 1935. A lesser-known component of the Social Security Act was the enhancement of federal oversight, and the requirement to audit almost all grant programs.

The next significant increase in grants came during President Lyndon Johnson administration's Great Society initiatives. Congress increased grants to state and local governments from 132 in 1960 to 387 in 1968. In 1965, possibly the second most well-known grant program, behind Social Security, came into existence. The Social Security Act Amendments of 1965 established Medicare, a hospital insurance program for people 65 and over, and Medicaid, a health insurance program for the poor. Within the first three years, almost 20 million people enrolled in Medicare alone. Today, Medicare has approximately 44 million people enrolled, about 15% of the population. In 2017, Centers for Medicare and Medicaid Services (CMS) estimated that about 74 million people were enrolled in Medicaid, with approximately 40 percent being children.

In the 1980s, President Reagan, a former governor of California, trusted the states to better provide essential government services instead of the federal government. This train of thought continued into the '90s during the Clinton presidency and was characterized by reforming several programs. Specifically, welfare became Temporary Assistance for Needy Families (TANF), and food stamps became the Supplemental Nutrition Assistance Program (SNAP). While they are two separate programs, they often go together—the funding for these programs is provided to the states as a block grant. The receiving state contributes their own funds and then manages the overall payout while adhering to the structure and guidelines set forth by Congress, mostly within their discretion.

In response to the Great Recession, which was officially classified as occurring from December 2007 to June 2009, President Barack Obama signed the American Recovery and Reinvestment Act of 2009 (ARRA). It aimed to help promote economic recovery and infrastructure investments, and aid state and local governments in offsetting reductions in services. The Government

Accountability Office's report to Congress titled: "Recovery Act: Grant Implementation Experiences Offer Lessons for Accountability and Transparency," indicates that as of October 2013, the federal government provided $812 billion for ARRA-related activities. Many of the ARRA grants stretched to an estimated end date of 2019 and a total overall outlay $830 billion from 2009-2019.

All Recovery Act funding

Grants, contracts, and loans

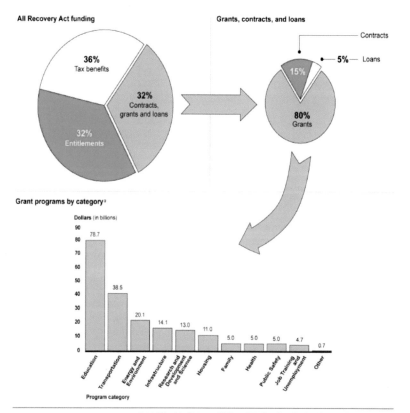

36%
Tax benefits

32%
Contracts,
grants and loans

32%
Entitlements

Contracts

15%

5% — Loans

80%
Grants

Grant programs by category [a]

Dollars (in billions)

90
80
70
60
50
40
30
20
10
0

78.7 — Education
38.5 — Transportation
20.1 — Energy and Environment
14.1 — Infrastructure
13.0 — Research and Development and Science
11.0 — Housing
5.0 — Family
5.0 — Health
5.0 — Public Safety
4.7 — Job Training and Unemployment
0.7 — Other

Program category

Sources: GAO analysis of Recovery.gov, U.S. Treasury Federal Agency Financial and Activity Reports and Recovery Act recipient reporting data.

I've spent over a decade working in the federal grants world. I've served as a junior Grants Management Specialist, a Grants Management Officer, a Policy Director, and most recently a Senior Analyst in the Executive Office of the President. My roles have varied, but my interest and passion for improving the federal grants experience and in public service has not! If you're like me, you're probably wondering what the federal grants world will look like in 2025 or 2030. No one knows for sure, but the public is generally united in the desire for it to be simpler and also more transparent. There is an obvious need to simplify the grants application process, streamline and simplify the grants financial management process, and ensure that we are using federal grants to perform services that actually provide a meaningful and measurable service to the public.

Several government initiatives were launched in 2018 to improve the federal grants process. OMB Memorandum M-18-24, Strategies to Reduce Grant Recipient Reporting Burden, details the government's effort to make significant changes to the grants management process to make things easier. You can review it here: https://www.whitehouse.gov/wp-content/uploads/2018/09/M-18-24.pdf.

The memo includes detailed approaches to reducing burden for grantees and increasing the government's focus on grant performance and outcomes, rather than on the completion of forms and reports. The memo also requires federal agencies to work together to reduce the number of grants systems that applicants and grantees have to use (there are currently at least 36 grants systems), and assess existing grant-making policies and business processes to figure out how to eliminate unnecessary or duplicate data collection. When the goals of this initiative of met, the grants world will be a better place.

Hopefully, with some modernizing and standardizing, the grants application process will allow anyone to quickly apply for a grant in a day or two vs. a month—maybe even in a couple of hours! And thus, this book will no longer be needed. How's that for a short-term goal?

You can learn more about the initiatives that are underway in 2019 here: www.performance.gov.

CONCLUSION

Many grant programs aren't well known and thus don't receive many applications from the public. This may be because the government doesn't do the best job marketing and/or because the application process is intimidating.

That shouldn't hold you back! You now have the scoop on where to look and even how to have NOFOs emailed to you. You know where to sign up, and you have an idea of what you'll encounter along the way.

Spend some time considering how your organization can serve the needs of the public. I'd also recommend that you occasionally search the Grants.gov website to see what NOFOs are out there; that may cause some ideas to pop into your mind.

There are lots of programs that may inspire you to try something new or give you an idea of how you can meet a public need that you didn't know existed.

Out of curiosity, for example, I searched the keyword "homeless" and found a few interesting programs:

- ✔ Youth Homelessness Demonstration Program

- ✔ Transitional Living Program and Maternity Group Homes

I then searched keyword "wilderness" and found:

- ✔ Upper Salmon Basin Habitat Improvement Planning and Coordination

- ✔ Improving Habitat Quality in Oregon Big Game Migration Corridors

There are all kinds of opportunities out there. The programs under each keyword have a unique focus, and yet they could potentially be won by one organization.

Good luck with your search!

Commonly Used Grants Terms

Closeout Process

The administrative process that must be followed at the end of a grant project. This includes the submission of a final report.

Discretionary Grant

A discretionary grant is the same as a competitive grant; it is a grant that is awarded based on a competition.

Notice of Award (NOA)

Document notifying you that you are being awarded a grant.

Fiscal Year

The government's financial business year. The fiscal year begins October 1 and ends September 30.

Non-competitive Grant

Non-competitive grants are basically the same as mandatory grants; they must be awarded based on law or a government requirement.

Award Period

The phase that begins after your grant is awarded.

Pre-award Period

Typically, the 90-day period before you are issued a grant.

Project Period

The total length of a grant award. Potentially made up of multiple budget periods.

Online Resources

➤ Participate in free online federal grants training at this website: https://cfo.gov/grants/training/

➤ Join the Grants Management Community of Practice here: https://digital.gov/communities/results-oriented-accountability-for-grants/

➤ The Federal Grants Regulations can be accessed here: https://www.ecfr.gov/cgi-bin/text-idx?tpl=/ecfrbrowse/Title02/2cfr200_main_02.tpl

➤ Keep an eye on government-wide grants initiatives at www.performance.gov.

➤ Check out the Grants.gov "Getting Started" page for basic grant information: https://www.grants.gov/web/grants/applicants/apply-for-grants.html.

➤ Here's a helpful page with information and sample research grant applications: https://www.niaid.nih.gov/grants-contracts/sample-applications

➤ For a look at the cornerstone of the grants universe, read: Federal Grant and Cooperative Agreement Act of 1977

➤ For ideas about Risk Management and Internal Controls check out the Government Accountability Office's "Green Book": https://www.gao.gov/greenbook/overview

➤ For details on specific grants programs browse the Assistance Listings: https://beta.sam.gov/search?index=cfda

➤ OMB Circular No. A-123 defines management's responsibility for internal control in Federal agencies. Take a look: https://obamawhitehouse.archives.gov/omb/circulars_a123_rev/

➤ To look through a repository of federal terms and definitions visit the online CDER Library here: https://repository.usaspending.gov/cder_library/

ACKNOWLEDGEMENTS

This book would not have been possible without the incredible group of people who make up my inner circle. Without each of you, I would not have been able to achieve my dream of sharing this message with the world.

Thank you,

Dennis Dantro, my best friend. Layla, Julian, and Adrian, for your infinite love. Mahasin, Mummina, Zainab, Rubayyi, Deloria, Gina and Sana, for the joy of sisterhood. Tina and Dennis, for being the world's greatest and most generous in-laws. Kate, Christy, Kisa, Chioma, Emeka and Xanthia, for being my forever friends.

Quadira served as the Director of the Office of Grants Policy, Oversight and Evaluation at the Department of Health and Human Services (HHS). While there, she was responsible for the development and implementation of regulations, policies, and procedures relating to HHS's grants programs. She also spent much of 2018 and 2019 at OMB where she led in the implementation of the President's Management Agenda Cross-Agency Priority Goal titled: "Results-Oriented Accountability for Grants." Quadira has held management positions at the National Institutes of Health, the Department of Defense, and the Department of Labor. Quadira has more than 15 years of experience solving complex business and financial management problems, driving large-scale change management initiatives, and administering sizeable financial assistance management operations. Quadira is a Navy Veteran and a Certified Research Administrator.

Made in the USA
Coppell, TX
21 September 2020